Festival City

A Pictorial History of the Edinburgh Festivals

THE SCOTSMAN presents

Festival City

A Pictorial History of the Edinburgh Festivals

Foreword by Alexander McCall Smith

Introduction by John McLellan, Editor in Chief,
The Scotsman Publications Ltd

With thanks to Craig Nelson and the library staff of
The Scotsman Publications Ltd

breedon **books**
PUBLISHING

Supporters

Absolutely Legless

S.C.D.A. (Edinburgh) Library

Michael J. McLean

Dr. Janet Henderson

Gordon Hughes

Tracey Parkinson

Mark Steinmann

John Dunn

George Glen

Gerald Dunlop

Alan Smith

Mrs Jeanette Scott

John M. Andrew

Dr. Angus McGregor

The Lady Sempill

Vanburgh

ne MacIntosh - Van Heel

Anne Gillingham

Robert Banks

First published in Great Britain in 2009 by
The Breedon Books Publishing Company Limited
Breedon House, 3 The Parker Centre,
Derby, DE21 4SZ.

A catalogue record for this book is available from the British Library.

ISBN 978-1-85983-739-9
Printed and bound by MKT Print, Slovenia.

Contents

Acknowledgements

The images contained in this book are testimony to the skill and dedication of the staff photographers of The Scotsman Publications Limited, both past and present.

Photographers vie for prime position during the 1964 Edinburgh International Festival.

Foreword

There is something compelling about press photography. Newspaper photographers have an eye for the important moment; they have, I suspect, a heightened sense of the dramatic. This photographic record of the Edinburgh festivals, drawn from the library of that great Scottish institution *The Scotsman* newspaper, has all the immediacy and atmosphere of newspaper photography. These photographs all have something of the liveliness and excitement of the events they record.

And what a story they tell! The foundation of the Edinburgh International Festival came only a few years after the end of World War Two. The continent of Europe was in ruins and Britain was rundown and exhausted by the conflict. Humanity had shown itself capable of appalling savagery – no surprises there, perhaps – and the very foundations of European culture had been called into question. In one sense it was a bad time to start an arts festival; in another it was exactly the right time to do so.

Over the 60 years that have followed that first festival, August in Edinburgh has become an increasingly

Musical instruments and names of composers are illustrated in the Floral Clock in Princes Street Gardens in 1947 to commemorate the first year of the Edinburgh International Festival.

important fixture in the world's cultural year. The growth of the Fringe and the spilling over of all sorts of artistic events into all sorts of venues has made the whole occasion a triumphant flowering of the artistic spirit. And this flowering is open to all; this is no solemn rehearsal of the accepted canon, this is a riotous explosion of all forms of art, offering something for virtually everybody. And a glance at these pages confirms that: celebrated conductors rub shoulders with frothy celebrities; street artists perform outside while inside audiences enjoy opera or ballet; families enjoy the slick pageantry and display of the Tattoo, while student thespians entertain their audience with perhaps not the best rehearsed contemporary drama.

And as a backdrop to all this there is this extraordinary city. I have sometimes thought that living in Edinburgh is like living on an opera set. The city is an intensely romantic one, and this romance is well-captured in these photographs. Look at the details. Look at the buildings in the background, at the clothing and at the cars in the street. Look at the bearing and appearance of the performers. These photographs reveal a great deal not only about what was happening artistically, but about what was happening in the world at the time.

Coming to the end of this book, I felt that I had been given a glimpse of something rather touching. Why? Because this is a photographic record of a love affair – between a city and the artists it nurtures and hosts. It has been a long-lasting love affair, and it is by no means over yet.

Alexander McCall Smith

Introduction

If anyone was ever in any doubt about the international importance of Edinburgh's festivals, they need only take the briefest of glances through the pages of this book.

World stars like Orson Welles, Richard Burton and Gene Kelly have made their way to Scotland in August to be part of what remains the world's greatest artistic gathering, to see not only the finest performers at the peak of their powers, but also to glimpse those about to emerge. Scotsman Publications' photographers have caught scores of stars on camera over the past 60 years and this wonderful collection stands as testament to Edinburgh's place as the test bed for talent in Scotland, the UK and beyond throughout that time.

Welles, Burton and Kelly are here in this book, along with other global stars like Margot Fonteyn and Rudolf Nureyev, rubbing shoulders with up-and-coming youngsters like Ian McKellen, Billy Connolly, Rowan Atkinson and John Hurt. Nowhere else in the world have so many well-known performers from so many disciplines assembled in one place to celebrate the arts for so long.

Of course, the rest of the world has woken up to what the festivals have done for Edinburgh and, with competition now fierce – even Leicester has a burgeoning comedy festival – the city and its creative community face a considerable challenge to keep the city ahead of its rivals. But Edinburgh has proved up to the challenge and with leadership and imagination there is no reason why the Edinburgh festivals will not remain at the centre of world creative calendars for many years to come.

John McLellan, Editor-in-Chief,
The Scotsman Publications Ltd.

Rudolf Bing (right), the first Artistic Director of the Edinburgh International Festival, is met at Turnhouse Airport by his successor Ian Hunter and Mrs Hunter in 1954.

Film Festival

Actor and director Orson Welles arrives at the Cameo Cinema during the 1953 Film Festival to give a lecture in which he declared that 'the film industry is dying'.

Film star Joan Bennett signing the visitors' book at the City Chambers in 1954, watched by Lord Provost Banks, Argentine Ambassador Dr Derisi, her film producer husband Walter Wagner, and the Lady Provost.

Denis Forman, director of the British Film Institute, and actor Michael Redgrave, who gave a lecture at the Cameo Cinema in 1954.

Film producer Betty Box, director Ralph Thomas and actor Dirk Bogarde read the programme for the 1955 Film Festival at a reception in the Film House in Hill Street.

Matsutarō Kawaguchi and Vittorio de Sica receive awards from Douglas Fairbanks Jr. at the 1955 Golden Laurel awards ceremony at the New Victoria Cinema in Clerk Street.

Scottish entertainer Duncan Macrae and French director and actor Jacques Tati at a reception at the Film House in 1955.

Gene Kelly in the Film House to open the 1956 Film Festival. The Queen attended a showing of his film *Invitation to the Dance* at the New Victoria Cinema.

Mr Forsyth Hardy, Honorary Secretary of the Edinburgh Film Festival, talks to actors Kenneth More and Muriel Pavlov at the Playhouse at a special presentation of *Reach for the Sky* in 1956.

Two Eliza Doolittles offer director Anthony Asquith a sprig of heather at a showing of *Pygmalion* to mark the Rank Organisation's 21st anniversary at the New Victoria Cinema in 1956.

Swedish actress Marta Toren admires the Golden Laurel award presented to film producer Sir Michael Balcon at the New Victoria cinema in 1956. Balcon was best known for his work at Ealing Studios. Sadly Marta Toren died the following year from a brain haemorrhage.

Terry Thomas with director John Boulting and his wife Anne at the White Cockade Club after the premiere of the film *Lucky Jim* in 1957.

Actress Melina Mercouri and director Jules Dassin at a reception at the Film House for the film *He Who Must Die* in 1957.

German film stars Barbara Frey and Horst Buchholz (who would go on to star as one of *The Magnificent Seven*) arriving at Turnhouse Airport in 1958.

French film stars add a touch of glamour to the 1958 Film Festival in the Film House. Left to right: Noelle Adam, Dominique Wilms, Nicole Berger and Nadine Tallier.

Swedish film actress Elsa Prawitz meets Gilbert the milk horse in 1963.

Herbert Lom and Gia Scala at the Film House in 1960. They attended the premiere of *I Aim at the Stars* at the New Victoria cinema.

Alan Bates and director Clive Donner attend the British premiere of their film *The Caretaker* in 1963.

Actor Ray Brooks at the Film House during the 1965 Film Festival for a showing of *The Knack ...and How to Get It*.

Wendy Craig does some sightseeing during a visit in 1966 for a gala performance of her film *Just Like a Woman*.

Director Samuel Fuller in Edinburgh for the 1969 Film Festival, which held a retrospective of his films.

Edinburgh Film Festival chairman Charles Oakley (left) presents American film director King Vidor with the first Golden Thistle award for outstanding achievement in filmmaking at the ABC cinema in 1964.

Peter Fonda attended a gala performance of *Easy Rider* in 1969.

Actor and director John Huston at the Film Festival for a showing of his film *Fat City* in 1972.

Chairman of 20th Century Fox Darryl F. Zanuck collects the Golden Thistle award at the Odeon Cinema in 1970.

Nick Nolte at the 1980 Film Festival to promote *Heart Beat*.

Annie Lennox attending a preview of the Eurythmics documentary *Brand New Day* in 1987.

Clint Eastwood at a press conference before the premiere of *White Hunter, Black Heart* in 1990.

Ewan McGregor at the premiere of *Velvet Goldmine* at the Odeon cinema in 1998.

Pierce Brosnan and Rene Russo arrive at the Odeon cinema for the European premiere of *The Thomas Crown Affair* as part of the 1999 Film Festival.

Kate Winslet makes her way through the rain to attend the party at the National Museum of Scotland to mark the premiere of *Enigma* in 2001.

Sigourney Weaver and Alan Rickman at the premiere of *Snow Cake* at the Dominion Cinema in 2006.

Charlize Theron at the party in 2006 to mark the 60th Edinburgh Film Festival.

Theatre

Eileen Herlie as Medea at the Lyceum Theatre in 1948.

Alan Badel as Romeo and Claire Bloom as Juliet in The Old Vic Company's production at the Assembly Hall in 1952.

Jean-Louis Barrault as Hamlet and Eleonore Hirt as Ophelia in La Compagnie Renaud-Barrault production at the Lyceum Theatre in 1948.

The world premiere of Christopher Hassall's *The Player King* by the Henry Sherek company at the Lyceum in 1952, starring Tony Britton (centre).

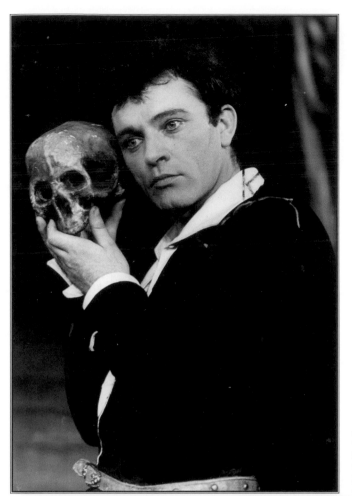

Richard Burton holds the skull of Yorick in the Old Vic Company's production of *Hamlet* in the 1953 Festival, where he starred with Claire Bloom as Ophelia (below).

Impresario Henry Sherek talking with Margaret Leighton, who was appearing in his production of *The Confidential Clerk* in 1953.

Stanley Holloway shows Moira Shearer the costume he will be wearing for the part of Bottom in *A Midsummer Night's Dream* at the Empire Theatre in 1954.

American actress Ruth Gordon with playwright Thornton Wilder before the premiere of Wilder's play *The Matchmaker* in 1954.

Eileen Herlie, Sam Levene and Ruth Gordon as Dolly Levi in Tennent Productions Ltd's *The Matchmaker* at the Lyceum in 1954. The play formed the basis for the musical *Hello Dolly*.

Louis Seigner (left) and members of La Comédie-Française, who presented *Le Bourgeois Gentilhomme* at the Lyceum in 1954.

Paul Rogers as Brutus and Wendy Hiller as Portia in the 1955 Old Vic Company's production of *Julius Caesar* at the Lyceum.

Tennent Productions Ltd presented *A Life in the Sun* by Thornton Wilder in 1955 with Irene Worth as Alcestis and Robert Hardy as Admetus.

French actress Edwige Feuillère in her company's production of *La Dame Aux Camélias* at the Lyceum in 1955.

Donald Houston, Diana Maddox and William Squire starred in the world premiere of the first professional stage production of Dylan Thomas's *Under Milk Wood* at the Lyceum in 1956.

Members of the Piccolo Teatro, Milan, in Goldoni's *Arlecchino: The Servant Of Two Masters* at the Lyceum in 1956.

Christopher Plummer in the title role of Henry V in the Stratford Ontario Festival Company's 1956 production.

Lennox Milne and Duncan Macrae in the Gateway Theatre Company's *The Flouers o' Edinburgh* in 1957.

Ernest Thesiger, Robert Eddison, Clare Austin and Robert Speaight from the Edinburgh International Festival group production of *The Hidden King* at the Assembly Hall in 1957. The verse drama received such scathing reviews that a public forum was held. Pictured below, Irish actor Micheál MacLíammóir speaks at the forum with fellow cast members sitting in front of him. Behind, left to right, are Stephen Mitchell, who presented the play, Edinburgh International Festival director Robert Ponsonby and the Countess of Roseberry, who presided over the forum.

The Ulster Theatre Group in Tyrone Guthrie's production of Gerald McLarnon's *The Bonefire* in the Lyceum in 1958.

Alan Bates, Ian Bannen, Gwen Ffrangcon Davies and Anthony Quayle in The New Watergate Theatre Company presentation of Eugene O'Neill's *Long Day's Journey into Night* in 1958.

A scene from the 1959 Edinburgh International Festival Company's production of *The Thrie Estaites* at the Assembly Hall.

In the production the Three Vices were played by James Gibson (Falsehood), Walter Carr (Deceit) and Duncan Macrae (Flatterie).

Moyra Fraser, Joss Ackland and Alec McCowen in the Old Vic Company's production of *The Double-Dealer* by William Congreve in 1959.

Patrick Magee as Father Domineer and Berto Pasuka as The Cock in the English Stage Company's presentation of Sean O'Casey's *Cock-a-Doodle Dandy* at the Lyceum in 1959.

Iain Cuthbertson in *The Wallace* presented by the Festival Society in the Assembly Rooms in 1960. The production's perceived partisanship proved controversial.

Mary Ewing, a member of the Scottish Patriots, presented Cuthbertson with a Lion Rampant flag at the end of one performance, which was followed by an audience rendition of Burns's *Scots Wha Hae*.

Tom Courtenay and Ann Bell in the 1960 Old Vic Theatre Company's production of *The Seagull*.

Peter Ellis as the Evil Angel in the Old Vic's 1961 production of *Doctor Faustus* at the Assembly Hall.

Albert Finney with John Moffatt in the English Stage Company's production of *Luther* at the Empire Theatre in 1961.

Paul Daneman plays Philip Faulconbridge with Maurice Denham in the title role in the Old Vic production of *King John* in the Assembly Hall in 1961.

The English Stage Company's production of *August for the People* at the Lyceum in 1961. Left to right: William Kendall, Cyril Raymond, Rex Harrison and Rachel Roberts.

Natasha Parry, Alec Guinness and Googie Withers starred in the English Stage Company's *Exit the King* at the Lyceum in 1963.

Dorothy Tutin in the 1962 Royal Shakespeare Company presentation of *Troilus and Cressida* at the Lyceum.

Richard Briers, John Hurt and Leonard Rossiter in *Hamp* at the Lyceum in 1964.

Jennie Woodford as Jaquenetta and Russell Hunter as Costard in the Bristol Old Vic production of *Love's Labours Lost* in 1964.

Watched by Victor Spinetti and Festival Director Lord Harewood, director Joan Littlewood faces the press after her production of *Henry IV* was heavily criticised. 'Critics,' she said, 'are like old ladies: they like what they have been used to.'

Director of the Moscow Puppets Sergei Obraztsov with 'the drunkard' during their appearance at the Gateway Theatre in 1966.

David Kincaid and Jean Taylor Smith in the Royal Lyceum Theatre Company's *The Burdies* in 1966.

Members of the Pop Theatre Company backstage in 1966. Standing on the windowsill are Tom Baker, Laurence Harvey and Jim Dale.

Jane Asher during the rehearsals of Pop Theatre's production of *The Trojan Women* in 1966, where she was the centre of attention due to her relationship with Paul McCartney.

James Earl Jones in
The Emperor Jones at
the Lyceum in 1967.

Cleo Laine as Titania
with Hywel Bennett
as Puck in the 1967
Pop Theatre
production of *A
Midsummer Night's
Dream* at the
Assembly Hall.

Ian McKellen triumphed at the 1969 Edinburgh International Festival with dual performances in Marlowe's *Edward II* (right) and Shakespeare's *Richard II* (pictured below, with Lucy Fleming as Queen Isabel).

Richard Howard, Maureen Pryor and Richard Wilson in a scene from *Would You Look At Them Smashing All The Lovely Windows* at the Church Hill Theatre in 1969.

The cast of the 1968 production of *The Resistible Rise Of Arturo Ui*. Left to right: Del Henney, Leonard Rossiter in the title role, Harold Innocent and Steven Berkoff.

Joanna Wake and Edward Fox in the 1971 Young Vic production of *The Comedy of Errors* at Haymarket Ice Rink.

Ian McKellen as Giovanni and Felicity Kendal as Annabella in the Actors' Company's production of *Tis Pity She's a Whore* at the Lyceum Theatre in 1972.

A scene from the Prospect Theatre Company's production of Shakespeare's *Pericles* in 1973.

Paul Jones, former singer with Manfred Mann, is threatened by the Devil, played by Peter Straker, in *Pilgrim*, a musical based on John Bunyan's *Pilgrim's Progress*, in 1975.

They are now best known for their television roles as Poldark and Taggart, but in 1974 Robin Ellis and Mark McManus starred in *The Bacchae* at the Assembly Hall.

Alan Rickman and Anna Calder-Marshall in the 1976 Birmingham Repertory Company's production of *The Devil is an Ass* at the Assembly Hall.

Edna Dore and J.G. Devlin as Mr and Mrs Noah in the National Theatre Company's 1980 production of *The Passion* at the Assembly Hall.

Peter Ustinov directed and starred in *The Marriage* in 1982.

David Rintoul as the King in the Scottish Theatre Company's 1984 production of *The Thrie Estaites*.

Alan Rickman and Beatie Edney in the Ninigawa Company's production of *Tango at the End of Winter* in 1991.

David Threlfall as Hamlet in the Oxford Playhouse Company's 1986 production of Shakespeare's play in the Assembly Hall.

One of the large-scale surreal images created by the Swiss mime group Mummenschanz in 1991.

Alan Stanford as King Herod with Olwen Fouere in the title role in the Gate Theatre production of Oscar Wilde's *Salome* at the Lyceum in 1989.

The History of the Horse, presented by the Gorky Theatre company of Leningrad in 1987 and starring Evgeny Lebedev.

The Catalan theatre group Els Joglars perform *Yo Tengo Un Tio en America* at the Lyceum in 1992.

Berlin's Hebbel-Theater in their production of *Dr Faustus Lights the Lights* at the Lyceum in 1993.

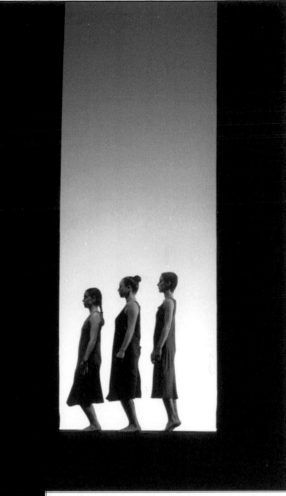

Ana Criado dances on the piano of Carles Santos during their 2001 production of *Ricardo I Elena* at the King's Theatre.

Peter Stein's seven-hour long production of Aeschylus' *Oresteia* at Murrayfield Ice Rink in 1994.

1994 saw the world premiere of *The Seven Streams of the River Ota* at Meadowbank Sports Centre.

Alan Cumming as Dionysus in the National Theatre of Scotland production of *The Bacchae* in 2007.

Christine Entwistle and friend in the Tron Theatre Company's production of *The Wonderful World of Dissocia* in 2004.

Fringe

More that is Fresh in Drama

By ROBERT KEMP

About this time we are all busy with fascinating, if pointless, comparisons between last year's Festival achievements and this year's prospects. To me it seems rather like asking which is better — the delicious cake you have just eaten or the cake which looks just as delicious but which you have not yet put in your mouth.

Certainly that is true of the dramatic confectionery. Last year we enjoyed the teamwork of the Old Vic in Shakespeare; this year we have no English classic, but instead one of the greatest actresses of the day, who happens to be a Scotswoman, in a modern re-creation of a Greek legend—Eileen Herlie in "Medea," directed by John Gielgud—so who is going to quibble? Last year we had the sardonic Jouvet in two French plays; this year we have the equally discussed French actor, Jean-Louis Barrault, in Andre Gide's translation of "Hamlet," an eighteenth-century comedy, and a mime, in which he specialises—again, who will complain?

Sound Choice

My own judgment would be that this year we seem lighter in the representation of the dramatic classics of almost schoolroom familiarity. There is much more that is fresh and that will ask us to make up our minds without the help of the preconceived notions which sometimes take charge as we watch the aforesaid classics.

Last year many people expressed the hope that the Scottish theatre would be given the chance to show what it could do, and the programme committee of the Festival decided that the first Scottish play should be Sir David Lindsay's "Satire of the Three Estates." I was asked to make an acting version of this long sixteenth-century work suitable for a present-day performance, so that I ought possibly to speak with some reserve about it.

I may, however, be allowed to express the view that the choice of the "Satire" was a sound one. Since I began to work upon it I have dipped into many histories of literature and drama out of curiosity to see what the learned authors say of it. I have yet to come across one who does not speak of it in the highest terms.

Reformation Factor

It is the first Scottish play in point of time, and is by general consent more interesting than anything produced in England at the same period. It has historical importance as a factor in the making of the Reformation in Scotland. Here one sees a Scottish writer influenced not by Calvin or Knox, but by the earlier reformer, Martin Luther.

The "Satire" was first performed before James V. at Linlithgow Palace in 1540, and later at Cupar, and then at the Greenside Playfield on the Calton Hill, Edinburgh. My task has involved the cutting of it

for length, and also, as someone wittily put it, for "breadth." The humour of those old days is of directness which would not be tolerated in these sly and sniggering modern times. I hope, however, that I have left in enough "breadth" to give something of the Rabelaisian flavour of the original.

That Lindsay was a true dramatic writer and not merely a poet seems to me beyond doubt. How amazing that in the sixteenth century he could find in Scotland some 4 actors to take speaking parts. That has not been possible again until to-day. An important fact to remember is that the "Satire" has been cast from Scottish actors earning their living here, the costumes designed by Molly MacEwen, now with the Glasgow Citizens, and the music written by Cedric Thorpe Davie, of St Andrews.

The presentation of the "Satire" is in the hands of Tyrone Guthrie

John Gielgud.

who as a young man was one of the early producers of the Scottish National Players, but who has since achieved international fame and is regarded as one of the few really great producers now at work. Lindsay's racy morality play could not be confined within the conventional stage, and in electing to play it in the Assembly Hall on an apron stage with the audience round three sides, Guthrie is not only conducting an important experiment but remaining true to the form of the piece. There will be no conventional scenery, the effect coming from the fine costumes and the plasticity of grouping possible on this kind of stage.

Round the Fringe

The Gateway, before assembling its own permanent company in the autumn, is given over to visits from two outstanding English companies — the Glyndebourne Children's Theatre in "Androcles and the Lion," by Bernard Shaw and Martin Browne's Pilgrim Players in "The First-Born," a new play, by the young English poet and playwright Christopher Fry on the subject of Moses.

Round the fringe of official Festival drama there seems to be more private enterprise than before. The Makars present the amusing Bridie skit on the Brains Trust and marriage, "It Depends What You Mean," in the Cygnet Theatre. In the Y.M.C.A. Christine Orr's company are giving the first performances of a new play by Robin Stark, "The Lady and the Pedlar," while later on Glasgow Unity bring a new comedy by Robert Maclennan, suitably entitled "The Flooers o' Edinburgh." I'm afraid some of us are not going to be often at home during the

nd Modern

justified—at least financially—in not increasing the proportion of concerts. This is the age of the star conductor and star soloists, and, among the latter, two great figures in the world of music are to be with us for a number of

The first use of the word 'Fringe' to describe the unofficial acts during the Edinburgh International Festival was coined by playwright Robert Kemp in his Festival preview in the *Evening News* on 14 August 1948.

Theatre Workshop present *Uranium 235* at the Oddfellowes Hall in 1951 as part of the Edinburgh People's Festival. At the top of the group is the playwright Ewan MacColl.

The Piccolo Company rehearse their 1954 production of *Mary Stuart* in Linlithgow Palace, the birthplace of Mary, Queen of Scots.

Craigmillar Castle provided a spectacular setting for a performance of *Edward II* by the Oxford University Players in 1954.

Jill Downes, Hilary Liddell and Edward Woodward in *The Queen and the Welshman* by the London Club Theatre Group in St Mary's Hall in 1957.

Simon Ward as Cressida and Richard Hampton as Troilus in the all-male Youth Theatre production of *Troilus & Cressida* at the Moray House Theatre in 1958. Both became successful actors and 20 years later Ward played Troilus in a National Theatre production.

Dudley Moore was one part of the Beyond the Fringe team who were a huge hit during the first week of the 1960 Festival. Showing his versatility, he returned a week later to play in a *Jazz at the Festival* concert.

A teenage Derek Jacobi played Hamlet in the all-male Players of Leyton production at Edinburgh Academy Hall in 1957.

A soldier at Edinburgh Castle is distracted as members of the 60 Theatre Group promote *The Captain's Hero* in 1963.

The 1963 cast of the Oxford Theatre Group revue, Robin Grove-White, Ian Davidson, Doug Fisher and future Monty Python member Terry Jones hold on to Jayne Braysham.

Stephen Frears receives the trophy for best university production in the 1963 Fringe on behalf of Cambridge University Theatre Company for their Barrie Theatre production of *Waiting for Godot*. Frears went on to direct such films as *Dangerous Liaisons*, *Mrs Henderson Presents* and *The Queen*.

Michael Palin and Terry Jones shoot it out in an open-air rehearsal for the 1964 Oxford Theatre Group's late-night revue.

Oxford Revue Group cast members Nigel Rees, Simon Brett, Mick Sadler and future political correspondent and *Strictly Come Dancing* contestant John Sergeant march over Diana Quick in 1966, who also took time out to brave the water at Portobello (above).

Members of Enfield Youth Theatre wear sandwich boards to promote their productions during the 1966 Fringe.

Glasgow University Dramatic Society present *Masque for 1966* in the Dunedin Lodge in Morningside.

Hildegard Neil and Chris Serle in *Ubu in Chains* at the Barrie Hall in 1967. The costumes were designed by Gerald Scarfe.

Backstage at the Corriefolk concert in 1966. The Corries are joined by actress and singer Marianne Faithfull.

Artist and promoter Richard Demarco with Clive James, who was directing the 1968 Cambridge Footlights.

Richard Stilgoe's one-man-band at the Richard Demarco gallery in 1970. A regular on television and radio, Stilgoe also wrote the lyrics for the musicals *Starlight Express* and *Phantom of the Opera*.

Fulton Mackay and Penny Casdagli in *Better Days, Better Knights* at the Pool Lunch Hour Theatre Club in Hanover Street in 1972.

Oxford Theatre Group presented *Fool's Paradise* in 1971, featuring Rosie Kerslake and Oz Clarke, who is now best known as a wine writer and broadcaster.

Hilary Westlake in *Pucka Ri* at Teviot
Students' Union in 1973.

Robert Bathurst and Carrie Simcocks from
the 1977 Cambridge Footlights revue at St
Mary's Hall.

The 'show must go on' spirit is epitomised by the Redbridge Drama Group, who continued their production of *Canterbury Tales* despite the roof falling in at the venue in 1977.

William Lindsay and Philip Franks in a scene from *Edward II* at the Little Lyceum in 1978.

Margo Upham in Stephen Sondheim's *Follies*, which had its British premiere in Portobello Town Hall in 1978.

Rowan Atkinson at Wireworks Theatre in July 1979 to assist in preparing the venue in time for the Fringe Festival.

Ann Scott-Jones and Frances Low in the Theatre Company's production of Tom McGrath's *Animal* at Moray House in 1979. Fourteen of the cast of 16 played chimpanzees and baboons.

Before Baldrick or *Time Team*, Tony Robinson appeared in *The Third Nam* by the Bristol Express Theatre Company in 1980.

Also with the Bristol Express Theatre Company in 1980 were Tony Allen and Alexei Sayle, who recently stated that 'Me and a guy called Tony Allen were the first stand-up comedy act to do Edinburgh. Everyone who came after that were our babies, and we'd like royalties, please.'

The cast of Circus Lumière, a circus show but for an adult audience, at the Meadows' Tent in 1980.

Cast of the 1981 revue *An Evening Without.* Left to right: Jimmy Mulville, Peter Fincham, Griff Rhys Jones, Martin Bergman, Rory McGrath and Clive Anderson.

Crowds pack the High Street for the first Fringe Sunday in 1981, which gave acts the chance to perform extracts from their shows.

The event proved so popular that it was moved to Holyrood Park and then to The Meadows.

Meera Syal won the award for the most promising actress of the 1983 Fringe.

Max Wall, comedian and actor, who read extracts from Samuel Beckett's *Malone Dies* in 1984.

Peyton Smith and Steve Buscemi in The Wooster Group production of *The Road to Immortality (part 2)* at the Church Hill Theatre in 1986.

Theatre de la Basoche performed their 1987 production *Le Lavoir* (The Laundry) in the Abbeymount washhouse.

Jo Brand poses with a model of a moon
fish at the Royal Museum of Scotland in
1988. She was known as 'The Sea Monster'
during her shows with Comic Abuse.

A 16-year-old Jude Law leads the
cast of the National Youth Music
Theatre's production of *Joseph
and the Amazing Technicolour
Dreamcoat* at Heriot Hall in 1989.

Russian actress Margarita Rasskazova in a production of Nikolay Karamzin's novel *Poor Liza* at the Traverse Theatre in 1989.

Spike Milligan made his Fringe debut in 1990 at the age of 72.

Future Labour Party leader John Smith, then Shadow Chancellor, joined writer and actor Stephen Fry to rehearse for a sketch in a comedy benefit show in 1990.

Comedian Sean Hughes with his 1990 Perrier Award. First awarded in 1981, the award became the most prestigious prize for the best comedy act at the Fringe.

Emily Woof hangs from a trapeze during a rehearsal of *Sex III* at the Bedlam Theatre in 1992.

A dancing Robson Green tries to impress Angela Lonsdale in the Northern Stage Company's production of *And a Nightingale Sang* in 1992.

In 1995 Teatr Biuro Podróży performed *Carmen Funebre* using masks, stilts and torches to create a memorable theatrical event in the playground of Drummond High School.

French-based Theatre Transformations in *C'est La Vie* at the St Brides Centre in 1997.

Gandini Juggling Project performing *Septet* at the St Brides Centre in 1997.

Jean Farrell promotes *Still Life* in 1998, a play about a woman who never moves.

Impressive flexibility shown by the stars of Circus Ethiopia, who appeared on Leith Links in 1998.

Italian mime artist Ennio Marchetto, whose quick-change act with paper costumes made him a Fringe favourite.

Arvaiden Theatre Company presents *Heaven's Mirror* at the Playhouse in 2000.

A dilemma for one of The Lady Boys of Bangkok, whose shows have been a Fringe sell-out for a decade.

Artists with light – Luma at the George Square Theatre in 2002.

Steven Berkoff during the recital of his own poem *Requiem for Ground Zero* at the Assembly Rooms in 2002. Berkoff has appeared at many festivals since the 1960s as an actor, director and writer.

Former rhythmic gymnastics champion Kristin Sroka performs with Vivace at the Famous Spiegeltent in 2003.

Bret McKenzie and Jemaine Clement of Flight of the Conchords were nominated for a Perrier Award in 2003.

Tanya Khabarova of the St Petersburg-based physical theatre company Derevo performs *Reflection* at St Stephen's Church in 2004.

Christian Slater as McMurphy in *One Flew Over the Cuckoo's Nest* at the Assembly Rooms in 2004.

The 'bath boy', David O'Mer, one of the performers from La Clique, whose mix of circus and burlesque has established it as a Fringe favourite.

Alan Davies and Bill Bailey in Neil Simon's *The Odd Couple* at the Assembly Hall in 2005.

A member of the Chinese State Circus has bricks smashed over his head during a performance in 2005.

One of the biggest hits of 2007 was *Fuerzabruta*, a theatrical spectacle involving aerial stunts and a swimming pool suspended above the audience.

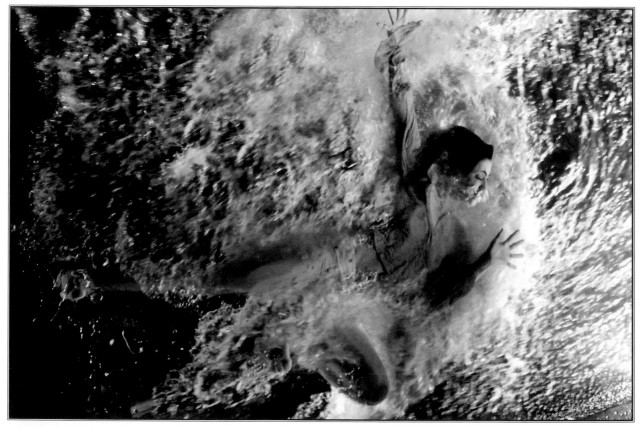

Recitals and Late Night Revues

Aberdeen-born opera singer Mary Garden, who gave a lecture in Central Hall during the 1952 Edinburgh International Festival.

In response to criticism of a lack of traditional Scottish culture, 1954 saw *Hail Caledonia*, a mix of singing, dancing and piping. The assembled choirs at the finale, with compère Roddy McMillan seated on stage.

Sir John Gielgud during a Shakespeare recital from the anthology *The Ages of Man* by George Rylands in the Freemasons' Hall in 1957.

Dame Edith Evans rehearses for a poetry reading entitled *A Recital of Verse and Music* at the Lyceum in 1958.

Dame Peggy Ashcroft rehearsing with Osian Ellis for their recital *Portraits of Women: From Chaucer to Dylan Thomas* at the Lyceum in 1958.

John Betjeman gave an afternoon poetry recital at the Lyceum during the 1959 Edinburgh International Festival.

Beatrice Lillie tests a new string of beads before her late-night revue at the Lyceum in 1960.

Grace Kelly, then Princess Grace of Monaco, appeared at the 1976 Edinburgh International Festival in a recital entitled *An American Heritage*.

French singer Juliette Greco performed a hugely successful week of late-night entertainment in 1961.

Marlene Dietrich and Burt Bacharach are mobbed by fans outside the Lyceum Theatre. Ms Dietrich was performing a series of late-night shows during the Edinburgh International Festival 1964 and was invited back the following year (pictured below, arriving at Turnhouse Airport, accompanied once again by Burt Bacharach).

Devisor John Carroll with actors Judi Dench and John Stride at a press conference before their 1978 recital of love letters called *The Language of the Heart*.

German singer Ute Lemper gave a late-night concert at the Festival Theatre in 1994.

In 1993 Jack Milroy, Jimmy Logan, Johnny Beattie and Walter Carr starred in *The Fabulous Fifties,* which recreated the famous Scottish variety shows of the past.

Royal Visits and Famous Visitors

Queen Elizabeth II and the Duke of Edinburgh in the Royal Box to watch the 1956 Tattoo.

Princess Margaret arrives at the Empire Theatre in 1956, where she attended a performance of *A Midsummer Night's Dream*. Accompanying her are Lord Provost John G. Banks and James Hill, manager of the theatre.

The Queen and Duke of
Edinburgh talk to Lord
Harewood after attending
a concert by the
Pittsburgh Symphony
Orchestra in the Usher
Hall in 1964.

Actress and singer
Ethel Merman visited
the Edinburgh
International Festival
in 1963.

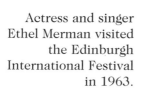

Actor Dick van Dyke points out the sights to his daughter Carrie Beth during a visit to the 1971 Edinburgh International Festival.

Actress Ingrid Bergman visits Edinburgh during the 1974 Edinburgh International Festival to see a performance by the Royal Stockholm Opera.

Princess Margaret caught theatre-goers by surprise when she arrived at the Lyceum Theatre just 10 minutes before the curtain for *You Can't Take It With You* in 1971.

Sean and Micheline Connery with their sons
Jason Connery (left) and Stephane Cosman
Connery, outside Richard Demarco's gallery
in the High Street in 1976.

Actor Burt Lancaster at the
Festival Club in 1976.

Peter O'Toole in the Caledonian Hotel in 1984. He was attending the festivals as patron of the Marmont Company to help launch their Fringe production.

Elizabeth Taylor watches the Edinburgh International Festival fireworks display with director Frank Dunlop in 1984.

The Scottish Play: Macbeth

Paul Rogers as Macbeth and Eric Porter as Banquo meet the Three Witches, played by Rachel Roberts, Clifford Williams and Job Stewart, in the 1954 Old Vic Company's production.

Ann Todd as Lady Macbeth in the same production.

Duncan Macrae as the porter in the Traverse Theatre production in 1965.

Mikijiro Hira as Macbeth and Komaki Kurichara as Lady Macbeth in the Toho Company's production of Shakespeare's play in traditional Japanese costume at the Lyceum Theatre in 1985.

John Kazek in Theatre Babel's 2004 version of the play.

Kathleen Broderick as Lady Macbeth and Richard Zeller as Macbeth in the 1999 Scottish Opera production of Verdi's opera at the Festival Theatre.

Members of Polish theatre company Teatr Biuro Podróży rehearse their unique interpretation of *Macbeth* in 2007.

Dance: Edinburgh International Festival and Fringe

The American Ballet Theatre perform *Themes and Variations*, choreographed by George Balanchine, at the Empire Theatre in 1950.

Curtain call for the Grand Ballet du Marquis de Cuevas' production of *Ines de Castro* at the Empire Theatre in 1952.

The New York City Ballet production of *Swan Lake* at the Empire Theatre in 1952.

Ballerina Margot Fonteyn on the steps of the National Gallery of Scotland in 1951.

Robert Helpmann as Oberon and Moira Shearer as Titania in The Old Vic Company's production of *A Midsummer Night's Dream* at the Empire Theatre in 1954.

Terence Longdon as The Soldier plays to the Princess, Moira Shearer, in the 1954 Old Vic Theatre Company's production of Stravinsky's *The Soldier's Tale*.

Azuma Kabuki dancers from
Japan at the Empire Theatre
in 1955.

Ballerina Svetlana Beriosova in
the 1956 Sadler's Wells Ballet
Company's *Birthday Offering*.

Michael Somes, Elaine Fifield and the Sadler's Wells Ballet Company rehearse for *The Miraculous Mandarin* at the Empire Theatre in 1956.

Ram Gopal Indian Ballet presented the world premiere of *The Legend of the Taj Mahal* at the Empire Theatre in 1956.

Viktor Fulop and Zsuzsa Kun
rehearse for the Hungarian
State Ballet production of
Swan Lake at the Empire
Theatre in 1963.

Gabriella Laratos leaps into
the arms of Andar Gal and
Zilany Gyozo in the 1963
Budapest Opera Company's
production of *The Miraculous
Mandarin* at the Empire
Theatre.

Members of the press assist Anita Cardus of the Stuttgart State Ballet, who had to withdraw after injuring her ankle during rehearsals in 1963.

Choreographer Alvin Ailey with members of his company at the Church Hill Theatre in 1968.

Anne Marie Vessel and Niels Kehlet in the Royal Danish Ballet's 1971 production of *The Lesson*.

Guest dancer Fernando Bujones has his kilt adjusted at the press preview of *La Sylphide*, presented by Scottish Ballet at the King's Theatre for the 1977 Edinburgh International Festival. He was joined in the production by Natalia Makarova (below).

A scene from the San Francisco Ballet production of *Romeo and Juliet* in 1981 at the Playhouse.

A dancer from Japanese company Sankai Juku in a scene from *Kinkan Shonen* at the Music Hall in 1982.

Dancers from the Xi'an Singing and Dancing Company from China, who gave an open-air performance of their 1987 show *The Soul of the Terracotta Army* at the Royal Scottish Academy.

The corps de ballet in the Matsuyama Ballet's production of *Giselle* at the Playhouse in 1988.

Indian dance–drama group Kathakali Theatre presented David McRuvie's adaptation of *King Lear* at the Lyceum in 1990.

A scene from the Ballet of the Deutsche Opera's 1991 production of *Ring Round the Ring* at the Playhouse.

Rudolf Nureyev as a bank clerk reminiscing about his past in the Cleveland San Jose Ballet production of *The Overcoat* in 1990.

The Mark Morris Dance Group at the King's Theatre in 1992.

The Royal Opera House and the Mark Morris Company present *Platée* at the Festival Theatre in 1997.

The San Francisco Ballet in its 1997 production of *Stravinsky's Violin Concerto*.

Patricia Barker dancing the role of Titania in the Pacific Northwest Ballet's 1998 production of *A Midsummer Night's Dream*.

Gerard Lemaitre and Martine van Hamel of the Nederlands Dans Theatre 3 (NDT3) in *Tears of Laughter* at the Playhouse in 1997.

A scene from the 2002 production of *Conjunto Di NERO,* choreographed and designed by Emio Greco and Pieter C. Scholten.

Laura Macias and Gavin De Paor of the Pasodos Dance Company pose on the roof terrace of the Museum of Scotland.

A dancer with the Materiali Resistenti Dance Factory of Italy in *Waterwall* in 2003.

Nataliya Shcherbakova in Bordeaux Opera Ballet's *Picasso and Dance* at the Playhouse in 2003.

Salt Lake City's Ririe-Woodbury Dance Company perform a retrospective of the work of choreographer Alwin Nikolais in 2004.

Pablo Sosa and Mariela Maldonado from Argentinian dance company Tango Fire during the 2005 Fringe.

In 2005 Scottish Ballet performed three works by George Balanchine at the Playhouse.

Jazz Festival

The Edinburgh Jazz and Blues Festival was founded by Mike Hart in 1978. Two of the first established jazz stars to play were saxophonist Benny Waters (pictured above) and trumpeter Teddy Riley (left) in 1980.

Although not officially part of the International Festival, two jazz legends played residencies in 1980: legendary jazz trumpeter Dizzy Gillespie (pictured above warming up before a concert) and saxophonist and club owner Ronnie Scott (pictured right).

The turning point in the Jazz Festival's success was the establishment of an opening parade. Above, a giant saxophone leads the way in 1982.

The Criterion Boys take part in the 1988 parade along Princes Street.

The parade now takes the form of a Mardi Gras-style celebration, ending in the Grassmarket.

Jazz pianist Teddy Wilson in 1982.

Van Morrison at the Playhouse in 2004.

Festival Conductors

Eduard van Beinum conducts the Concertgebouw Orchestra of Amsterdam in the Usher Hall in the opening concert of the 1948 Edinburgh International Festival.

Wilhelm Furtwängler conducting the Augusteo Orchestra in the Usher Hall in 1948.

Sir Adrian Boult with the London Philharmonic Orchestra at the opening concert of the 1951 Edinburgh International Festival at the Usher Hall.

Sir Malcolm Sargent conducts the BBC Symphony Orchestra in the Usher Hall in 1955.

Sir Thomas Beecham at the 1956 Edinburgh International Festival.

Ernest Ansermet and the Philharmonia Orchestra during a rehearsal for a concert in the Usher Hall in 1958.

Charles Mackerras rehearses with the Polish Radio Symphony Orchestra in 1962 under the watchful eye of composer Dimitri Shostakovich. In 2008 Mackerras was named the new Honorary President of the Edinburgh International Festival Society.

Sir George Solti conducts the orchestra of the Royal Opera House, Covent Garden, in the opening concert of the 1963 Edinburgh International Festival in the Usher Hall.

Sir John Barbirolli at the Press Bureau in 1965.

Herbert von Karajan conducted the Berlin Philharmonic Orchestra at the 1972 Edinburgh International Festival.

Yehudi Menuhin in 1953. A regular visitor to the Edinburgh International Festival, he was awarded the Freedom of the City in 1965 and was appointed the first honorary president of the Edinburgh International Festival Society in 1989.

William Foyle, soprano Elisabeth Schwarzkopf and actress Eileen Herlie in conversation at a Foyle's Literary Luncheon in the Caledonian Hotel in 1954.

Cellist Pierre Fournier, violinist Zino Francescatti and pianist Solomon rehearse before their recital at the Usher Hall in 1955.

Classical guitarist Andrés Segovia at the 1955 Edinburgh International Festival.

Dame Myra Hess rehearses with conductor Dimitri Mitropoulos before their concert with the New York Philharmonic Orchestra at the Usher Hall in 1955.

To try to expand the reach of the Edinburgh International Festival, a 'bob-a-head concert' was held at the Embassy Cinema in Pilton in 1958. Police had to turn away over 3,000 people from the concert by Caspar Cassado, Yehudi Menuhin and Louis Kenter (pictured left).

Festival personalities take part in a performance of Haydn's *Toy Symphony* in Freemasons' Hall. Left to right: opera singer Ian Wallace, Edinburgh International Festival director Lord Harewood, conductor Alexander Gibson, choreographer Leonide Massine, conductor Gennadi Rozhdestvensky and cellist Mstislav Rostropovich.

Russian composer Dmitiri Shostakovich attended the 1962 Edinburgh International Festival.

Yehudi Menuhin introduces Dr Narayana
Menon, who gave an illustrated talk on Indian
music at the Freemasons' Hall in 1963.

Cellist Jacqueline Du Pré, who made
her Edinburgh International Festival
debut in 1962.

Megaphones, vacuum cleaners, floor polishers
and rifles were among the 'instruments'
employed in the Hoffnung Concert in the Usher
Hall in 1968.

Tenor Charles Craig, cellist Mstislav Rostropovich and conductor Alexander Gibson before their recital at the Usher Hall in 1964.

Japanese musician and percussionist Stomu Yamash'ta searches through a scrapyard for items to use as instruments after his were left stranded by a rail strike in France in 1970. Yamash'ta played a concert with the Scottish National Orchestra.

Jazz violinist Stephane Grappelli in the capital for the 1973 Edinburgh International Festival. During his concert he invited a young pupil of Yehudi Menuhin's to join him on stage; 19 years later Nigel Kennedy returned to play a concert at Edinburgh Castle.

Opera singer Geraint Evans checks the damaged finger of pianist Daniel Barenboim. Barenboim had cut his finger on a broken mirror, almost causing him to miss the opening concert of the 1975 Edinburgh International Festival, but in the end the performance went ahead.

After retiring from concert and recital singing, Elisabeth Schwarzkopf returned to the Edinburgh International Festival in 1980 to give public master classes.

French sisters Katia and Marielle Labèque, who made their first Edinburgh International Festival appearance at the Queen's Hall in 1982.

Drama at the Drama Conference

One of the most controversial moments of the Edinburgh International Festival came on the last day of the 1963 International Drama Conference at the McEwan Hall.

During a debate on 'The Theatre of the Future', director Kenneth Dewey organised a 'happening' involving men appearing silhouetted in windows, the actress Carroll Baker clambering over seats, a gantry of death masks and a nude model called Anna Kesselaar being wheeled across the organ gallery. This caused a press furore, and indecency charges were brought against conference organiser John Calder and Miss Kesselaar, who was later acquitted while the charge against Calder was deserted.

Kenneth Dewey gestures towards the organ gallery.

American actress Carroll Baker clambers out of her seat.

Anna Kesselaar disrupts the International Drama Conference by whipping off her plastic mac and appearing nude on the organ gallery.

Opera

Mariano Stabile as Don Alfonso with two of the lovers in the 1948 Glyndebourne Opera production of *Cosi Fan Tutte* at the King's Theatre.

Hamburg State Opera Company in *Der Rosenkavalier* at the King's Theatre in 1952.

Hamburg State Opera also presented Wagner's *Die Meistersinger* the same year.

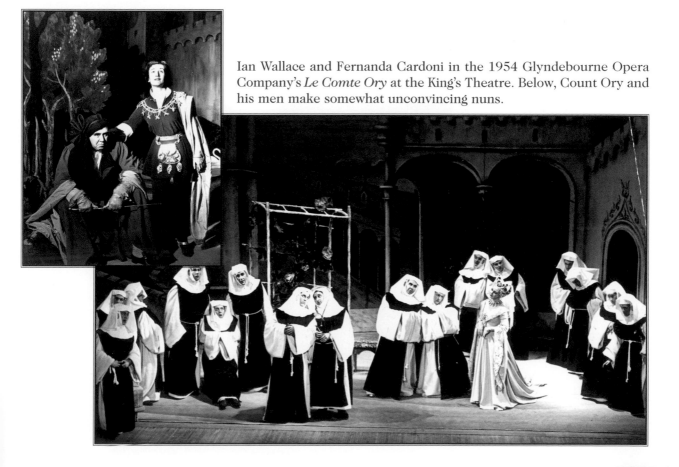

Ian Wallace and Fernanda Cardoni in the 1954 Glyndebourne Opera Company's *Le Comte Ory* at the King's Theatre. Below, Count Ory and his men make somewhat unconvincing nuns.

Fernando Corena as Falstaff in the 1955 Glyndebourne Opera Company's production at the King's Theatre.

Helmut Melchert as Oedipus in the Hamburg State Opera Company's *Oedipus Rex* in 1956.

Legendary opera singer Maria Callas arrives at Turnhouse Airport in 1957, where she was met by Edinburgh International Festival Director Robert Ponsonby. Ms Callas was appearing at the Edinburgh International Festival with La Piccola Scala opera company in a production of *La Sonnambula*.

Callas prepares for her role as Amina. She sang in the four performances she had been contracted to do, but when asked to do a fifth she refused, citing nervous exhaustion. A press furore followed after Callas left for Venice, but for her replacement, Renate Scotto, it proved to be a breakthrough performance.

Stuttgart State Opera Company present *Der Wildschutz* at the King's Theatre in 1958.

The Valkyries in a scene from Wagner's *Die Walkure* presented by the Royal Opera, Stockholm, at the King's Theatre in 1959.

Louis Quilico as Thoas in the
Covent Garden Opera Company's
production of *Iphigénie En
Tauride* at the King's Theatre in
1961.

Joan Sutherland in Covent Garden
Opera Company's 1961 production
of *Lucia Di Lammermoor*.

The 1963 Royal
Opera House
production of John
Gay's *The Beggar's
Opera* at the King's
Theatre, starring
Janet Baker.

Tony Ferrante as
Paris and Rita
Romanelli as Venus
dance in the
ballroom scene of
Teatro San Carlo's
presentation of
Adriana Lecouvreur
in the King's
Theatre in 1963.

Karlheinz Peters as Papageno the birdcatcher in the Wurttemberg State Opera production of *The Magic Flute* in the King's Theatre in 1966.

Fritz Linke and Gerhard Stolze in *Wozzeck* at the King's Theatre in 1966.

Patrick Wymark, Una Stubbs and Nicky Henson in the 1967 Scottish Opera production of Stravinsky's *The Soldier's Tale* at the Assembly Hall.

Tito Gobbi in the title role and Maddalena Bonifaccio as Lauretta in Puccini's *Gianni Schicci* at the King's Theatre in 1969.

During the 1975 Scottish Opera production of *Hermiston*, a doctor was on standby after Jim Hastie, who was suspended for around 15 minutes as the 'hanged man', passed out in rehearsal and after the first performance.

Geraint Evans as Figaro and Ileana Cotrubas as Susanna in *The Marriage of Figaro* at the King's Theatre in 1975.

James Maddelena and Carolann Page, as President Richard Nixon and First Lady Pat Nixon, land in Peking in the Houston Grand Opera's 1988 production of *Nixon in China* at the Playhouse.

President Nixon toasts Chinese premier Chou En-lai, played by Sanford Sylvan.

Bulat Minzhilkiev as Prince Ivan in *Khovanshchina* by the Kirov Opera in 1991.

The spectacular set for Baz Luhrmann's production of *A Midsummer Night's Dream* by Australian Opera at the Festival Theatre in 1994.

Scottish Opera's production of Bedřich Smetana's *Dalibor* at the Festival Theatre in 1998.

Karita Mattila in the 1998 Royal Opera House production of *Don Carlos* at the Festival Theatre.

Paula Delligatti in Royal Opera's 1998 production of Verdi's *I Manadieri*.

Die Zauberflöte was given a contemporary reworking by Festival d'Aix-en-Provence and the Opera National de Lyon in 2001.

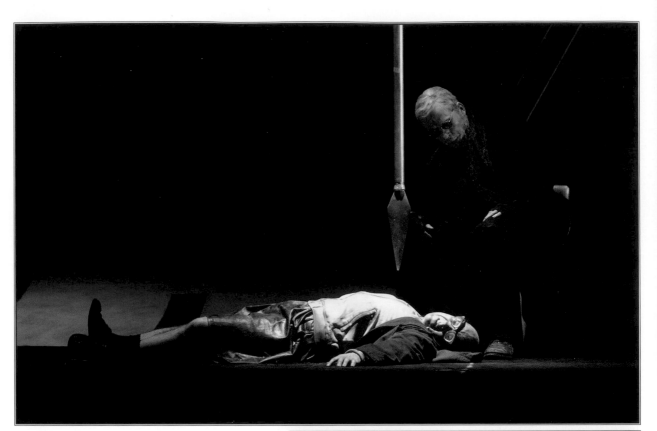

Alasdair Elliott and Matthew Best
in Scottish Opera's 2003 epic
production of the complete *Ring
Cycle* by Richard Wagner.

Hungarian soprano Erika Miklosa
as the Queen of the Night in *Die
Zauberflöte* in 2006.

Edinburgh – a City Transformed

The Cavalcade parade.

The traditional curtain-raiser is the Cavalcade parade involving performers from the Tattoo and the Fringe as well as pipe bands and local community groups.

Officials and dignitaries lead the procession up the Royal Mile to mark the official opening of the 1952 festivals.

Lantern-style decorations outside Jenners department store in Princes Street during the 1957 festivals.

Some of the cast from the 1958 Old Vic Company's production of *Mary Stuart* take a break from rehearsals in the Assembly Hall.

Opera fans queue outside the King's Theatre for tickets for *Lucia di Lammermoor* during the 1961 Edinburgh International Festival.

Illuminated decorations in Princes Street for the 1962 Edinburgh International Festival.

Spectators watching the fireworks display to mark the opening of the 1963 Edinburgh International Festival.

Children keep a safe distance from a group of camels sitting in Parliament Square as they await their cue to take part in the 1963 Tattoo.

Marillyn Gray as Cleopatra, accompanied by her hand-maidens, is the centre of attention as they promote *Toccata for Cats* at the Pollock Hall in 1963.

Raymond Duncan, brother of the dancer Isadora Duncan, attracts some attention as he walks along George Street during the 1963 International Festival. The previous year he had been voted one of the world's best-dressed men.

Harmonica virtuoso Larry Adler
gives an impromptu performance
to an appreciative audience outside
Morton House on Blackfriars Street
in 1965.

Two giant performers from the Road
Troupe theatre production of *Le
Morte d'Arthur* take the show to the
High Street in 1970.

Some local children chat with actor Timothy West in his costume as Dr Johnson in the West Port, 1970.

Children join clown and mime artist Bob Berky as he takes Tweed the dog for a walk in 1977.

Patrick Malahide and Tammy Ustinov take to the Edinburgh streets dressed as robots to promote *The Android People* in 1978.

A Fringe-goer greets a tree promoting the Bristol Reunion's show outside the Fringe office on the High Street.

Robin Strapp in the costume that secured him the 1981 Fringe Marathon competition. Robin managed 20 shows in 24 hours.

Japanese dancers from the Sankai Juku company in 1982 with their outdoor performance called *Sholiba* (a title taken from the butcher's trade and the hanging of meat). They are hanging from what was then the Lothian Regional Chambers on George IV Bridge.

A road sweeper stops to admire a chalk drawing of the *Mona Lisa* on the pavement outside the Royal Scottish Academy.

The Smallest Theatre in the World presents *A Tale of Two Cities* in 1984.

Two Fringe-goers seem unaware of the gruesome scene behind them provided by the cast of *Dr Cadavers* in 1984.

American artist Vera Simons created an inflatable sculpture for the National Gallery of Scotland during the 1986 Edinburgh International Festival, although it had to be deflated after a few days due to high winds.

A two-headed creature from The Open Hand Theatre Tickling Machine theatre workshop waits at a Stockbridge bus stop.

Stefan Depont from the French circus troupe Archaos drives a motorbike over a car on The Mound as a publicity stunt for their show in 1989.

Scottish artist George Wyllie perched on *A Temple for a Tree* – a 12ft high 'paper temple' in Princes Street Gardens in 1992. It survived for most of the festivals, until vandals set fire to it.

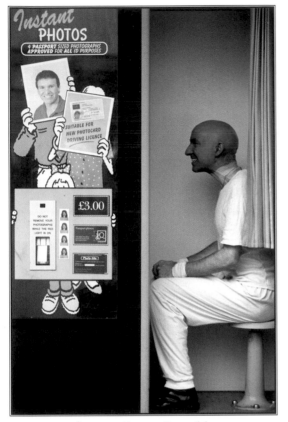

Fringe performer Bjorn Patzold gets some souvenir photographs.

Living statues such as this Statue of Liberty have become a regular sight on the streets of Edinburgh during the Festivals.

All Fringe performers are entitled to a coffee break.

Leyla Gencer visits the Palace of Holyroodhouse in her guise as Mary, Queen of Scots, whom she played in Donizetti's *Maria Stuarda* in 1969.

From the cast of Boswell's *Life of Johnson*, Timothy West as Dr Samuel Johnson, Julian Glover as James Boswell and Henry Moxon as Lord Auchinleck outside Boswell's Court in 1970. The close once gave entry to Auckinleck's house, where Boswell wrote his *Life of Johnson*.

Exhibitions and Visual Art

The 1954 *Homage to Diaghilev* exhibition at the Edinburgh College of Art commemorated Russian arts promoter and ballet impressario Sergei Diaghilev. Miss D. Sharp puts finishing touches to the Sleeping Beauty exhibit.

Princess Mary, the Princess Royal and ballerina Alicia Markova attend the opening of the exhibition.

Margot Fonteyn admires one of the posters in the exhibition.

St Michael and the Devil above the Waverley Market, promoting the Jacob Epstein Memorial Exhibition during the 1961 Edinburgh International Festival.

Incke Mater takes a seat among the giant fungi at an exhibition of prints by Salvador Dali on show at Pool Theatre Club in 1971.

Members of the Scottish Ballet recreate the Degas painting *The Ballet Class* to launch the 1979 exhibition *Degas 1879* at the National Gallery of Scotland.

A statue by Henry Moore looks out to the castle from the Royal Botanic Gardens.

The 1983 *Vienna 1900* exhibition was opened by Nuria Schoenberg Nono, daughter of the composer Arnold Schoenberg. Here she admires a portrait of her father by Alban Berg.

The Scotsman Steps Art Exhibition was a regular feature for many years. Above, actor Laurence Harvey opens the 1966 exhibition.

Edinburgh Military Tattoo

A matinee performance
of the 1952 Tattoo on
the esplanade of
Edinburgh Castle.

Royal Scots, in mid-
17th-century pikeman's
uniform, rehearse at
Glencorse Barracks for
the 1955 Tattoo.

A Highland dancing display in 1953.

The Spahis, cavalrymen from French North Africa, in the 1959 Tattoo.

Soldiers of the Scottish regiments dance a Foursome Reel in 1959.

The Barbados Police Force Band in 1964.

A spear dance by the soldiers of the Fijian Military Forces in 1965.

Members of the Royal Brunei Malay Regiment in a wooden boat called a prau, given a realistic look by the heavy rains that fell during this 1970 performance.

An RAF police dog gets a ride on his handler's bicycle in 1970.

A gymnastic and physical training display by RAF personnel from the PT school at St Albans in 1974.

The Sbandieratori dei Rioni di Cori, a traditional flag-waving display from Italy, in 1976.

Members of the Berlin Brigade Drill Team from the United States of America in 1976.

The cleaning crew stand by to clear up after the Irish Hunters from the band of the Blues and Royals in 1993.

The Tattoo has not been without moments of unscheduled drama. Above, a soldier pulls the burning canvas away from the spectator seating after a fire broke out during the 1957 dress rehearsal. No one was hurt in the incident.

The damage caused to a vaulted toilet block in the castle after two explosive devices went off during a performance in August 1971, injuring three people.

Piper Major David Black, the lone piper in 1966, is attached to a safety rope in case of high winds.

In 1978 there was a rehearsal to lower the lone piper in by helicopter for the matinee performance; however, he was lowered too far and had to clamber over the ramparts.

A war dance by Zulus from the South African Police Service in 1996.

A display of Highland dancing in 2000.

Maori Dancers from the the Ngati Rangiwewehi Group in 2000.

The Traditional Band and Dancers of the Republic of Korea in 2003.

The Military Band of the People's Liberation Army of China in 2004.

A dancer from the Russian State Cossack Song and Dance Ensemble in 2001.

The traditional finale of the lone piper.

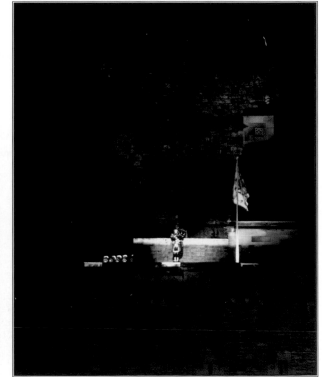

The pipes and drums of the Royal Caledonian Society of South Australia in 2007.

The massed pipes and drums at the 2006 Tattoo.

Book Festival

Three-year-old Catherine Blackwood meets a giant puffin at the first Book Festival in 1983.

A girl reads her book leaning against a model of the world's tallest man, Robert Pershing Wadlow, in 1985.

The Book Festival attracts the finest writers from both home and abroad. Edwin Morgan, 2000.

Dame Muriel Spark, 2004.

Doris Lessing, 1993.

Salman Rushdie, 2005.

Iain Banks, 2003.

At the opening event of the 2008 Book Festival, Ian Rankin interviewed the Prime Minister, Gordon Brown, about his book, *Courage: Eight Portraits*.

Fireworks

The end of the Edinburgh International Festival is signalled by the traditional, spectacular firework display when over 200,000 people fill the city centre and surrounding areas to watch and listen to the concert from the Ross Bandstand in Princes Street Gardens.

Fabulous Historic Memorabilia from

THE SCOTSMAN